Love-Noise

Poems

Elizabeth Twiddy

Standing Stone Books
Syracuse • Brussels

Love-Noise

Love-Noise: Copyright © 2010 by Elizabeth Twiddy

First Printing

Standing Stone Books is an imprint of **Standing Stone Studios**, an organization dedicated to the promotion of the literary and visual arts.

Mailing address:

951 Comstock Avenue, Syracuse, New York 13210 U.S.A.
and
Jesserenstraat 58, 3840 Borgloon, Brussels, Belgium

Email: info@standingstonestudios.org

Web address: www.standingstonestudios.org

Standing Stone Books are available in both print and ebook formats.

Printed by Versa Press, Inc., 1465 Spring Bay Road, East Peoria, Illinois 60611

ISBN 978-0-979-1944-5-0

Library of Congress Control Number: 2010934927

Set in Baskerville typeface, designed by John Baskerville

Cover and Text Design: Adam Rozum

Standing Stone Books is a member of the Council of Literary Magazines and Presses.

[clmp]

Love-Noise

for my family

Contents

IV

V

Introduction by Brooks Haxton

I am tempted, because Elizabeth Twiddy's writing moves me, to compare her to fine poets I already know. The electricity here has such an incandescence, it could be resurgent voltage from Emily Dickinson in distress, juiced up with an animal charge from D.H. Lawrence, and amplified in an oddball dynamo designed by Stevie Smith.

But Twiddy doesn't really sound like them, and how she sounds, her cadence, is the core of her effect, even in poems where the simplest language comes straight on, as it often does, in "Panic," for example:

Night rain falls on grass
in the still cemetery
where moths still flicker.

The flickering presents panic as a variation on "butterflies in the stomach," but with moths in a cemetery, in the rain, at night. The emotional concept is a vivid picture, but the essence of the poem involves rhythm too, with slow monosyllables at the opening and toward the end, and with quicker strokes of less stressed syllables between. This handling of inflection, in image and in sound, makes panic come alive.

For a poet this alert to nuance, older forms that heighten repetition are especially fitting. Sestina, rondel, pantoum, and more impromptu repetitions help to make the drama of essential transformation more distinct.

At the opening of the collection when we see "one of God's damp servants," a monarch butterfly, "throb with pungent glory," we take this neither as the emblem that it might have been for a more rhetorical writer, nor the object of a naturalist's dogged representation. Any animal in these poems, wasp, or pigeon, or opossum, is anima revealed, the soul, an apparition—maybe winged, but not because it is transcendent: it is always the genuine psyche, fraught with all the freight of flesh and mind.

What haunts the whole book, in the surge and aftermath of eros, in the empathy for family and for strangers, and in jolts of recognition, and of being recognized, is an imagination deeply and disturbingly alive, and tender to the touch.

Love-Noise

I

The Monarch

The monarch
flapped in the open yard, large,
pulsing as a ghost,
no more to me than an ordinary insect,
dying, almost unnoticed
with the other darting spirits
by the waxy pachysandra,
rapidly consumed by the earth.

I was astonished
to see, one night,
a filter of light
sift through its dusty wings,
and to think that the monarch,
floating between the dewy
buds of the red roses,
was transformed
into one of God's damp servants.

For life
it siphons nectar from milkweed
until its last swimming sweep
as it lights onto the cold sill of my room
to watch and throb with pungent glory.

In my room,
over a bed bleached white, stretched taut,
my family hovers. They shuffle and need faith.
When sun oozes in, all morning
they sit and wait to strike
like black ants
surging over a dying insect.
They peer over the edge of my bed:
sip their juice.

What is a Woman

What is a woman, if her chief good
is to burrow into the earth
like a blue mole, searching for the dead,
with no sense for the present, for the living?
Look how she noses around down there,
sifting her body into the silt
of the past, stubbornly, with no light,
completely ignoring the life above her.
She has questions for the dead ones—questions
she thinks necessary to this life.
Above her, the living wait.
They thunder the earth with their pacing:
bake bread, sing, plant seeds
in the garden: terrifying love-noise.

Blood, Glass, Pigeons in the Bathtub

The pigeons flap in the eaves below the window——
Loud! guttural warbles, overlapping, urgent,
piercing, like sharp-tongued human squabbling. I pound
the window glass with one palm, hoping to scare them
into flying away. But glass shatters,
and my hand is through the glass to the wrist——long silence
from shatter, the three-story fall, til the plates hit the ground.
Now glass in the tub, beneath the window. Now blood.
Now the ink-blue square of no-window. Now the threat
of the pigeons, coming right in, to strut in the tub.
The flaps of their wings outside, now deathly,
rise, as if to carry me off——the sifting sound, dissolving
the stuff of air, into——where? As if there were
some crime here——suspicion of blood and glass
in the bathtub, with pigeons standing dumbly around.
But truth: the angry sounds of the birds made me angry,
and I smashed the window——then what of the girl
in the hospital psych unit, who took the cardboard
out, leaving a black square next to the air conditioner,
and squeezed her body through——three stories,
she fell: a black sea wrapped in a white sail.

The Sparrow

I was pushed from the light
into dark through a hole.

My wet body hit the pavement
with a single thud.

I left my stain with the others'——thrush
of shadows among blood maple leaves.

Once, I flew toward home——
the white heat singed my feathers.

Their eyes peer through holes in the dark:

Which one of those beings filled with terrifying
light cast me out?

the Relativity of Nothing

even Nothing
is relative—with its
extinct
dinosaurs, its
black holes,
its tin slits in jail windows—
the distinctly
vaporized sense
of human ash in an oven, with
a wedding band
in a cake of soap bubbles in
the next room, a bathroom—
a bird stopped still
in flight—Nothing,
with its absence
of expected function—
a static bird, un-flying

Anorexia

              What I want
is to be invisible——spirit,
watching. But I am here: still
visible. I will be as small
as possible——silent, inside
myself, in communion
with God, secretly carrying
the power to perfect
inside my ribcage, like light:
the skeleton exposed, illumined.

Reflective

My little bowl of broccoli
will not talk to me:
It pains me to see
my little bowl of broccoli
with all its heads, sick green,
mirroring, mimicking me:
My little bowl of broccoli
will not talk to me.

April Heat

I felt ugly today so I stayed inside.
Outside my windows, wasps and hornets
clung to the panes. Because I couldn't rely
on the screens and storms, I kept
the frames sealed——too hot
inside, no air, but safe
from all the stinging things. Later,
one buzzed near the ceiling.
I trapped it.
With my sweaty yellow rubber-gloved
hand, I clasped the translucent tupperware
to the wall around it, tipped it
inside, then swiftly capped the top.
How beautiful it was, its legs
and all its tiny
hairs, lowering its wedge-face
to clean its antennae——then the thin wings
vibrating, suspending its body,
afloat in the small space,
an angel with string legs hanging.
I looked a long time at its face.
I wanted to explain my fear
of being stung; to apologize
for trapping it this way.
And I thought: My own face
scares me.
I'm afraid of being seen.

Making My World of Cut-Paper Dolls

after Popa and Simic

1. The Box

i have a little box
that is myself
with as many mirrors
making as many fractions of views
as possible—infinity—
infinitesimal—
with all its glass
edges exposed—

i have to be careful
not to cut things
as i examine
these infinite splits
of the world—
a naked light bulb hangs by a thread
in the center of the box—

2. Memory Makes the Box

Memory
practicing its scissor-clips
in the dark—
My Memory
taking its sleep-walking foot-steps—
picking and choosing
opening and closing the lids
of all the old boxes—
those boxes of dolls,
those cut-paper dolls—

3. Inside the Box: the Ballerina Box

In one little box
there is a ballerina
with pink toe shoes—
she spins
as a tune plays
until I shut the lid.

Sometimes,
in my dreams,
she comes to me and confides
she wishes I'd keep
her lid shut, so she can hide
in the quiet, in the dark.

4. Inside the Box: the Live Mannequin

Here I am,
in the store window—
boxed in glass.
I'm still, and silent,
but if you look closely
you'll see my heart beating faintly
with the slight quiver
of the covering cloth:
my visual is loud, calling:
Here I am.

II

There

they were all there
in the rooms
between floors
in the house

there, time was still
but the paintings moved
in and out
of rooms
and their faces
carried with them

Red Balloon

Untie the balloon from its black rail—
the child will weep with sudden loss
increasing with the rapid rise of the helium-
filled orb. All day
the clouds congeal and darken. Ants
appear, carrying their great bundles
across the cement, then disappearing—
and the child wonders where they go.
That night on his pillow, his head feels heavy,
cradled in the cool white bowl of it.

The End of Sleep

The eyes are about to open.
Through fog, Sleep crosses the great water——
See how it sails in the little boat?
Slowly, such a long journey,
Bits of light
Catch colors in the mirrored hull.
Beneath the glassy surface, a glimpse
Of your dreams: the lake, the boat, with you
In it. Now a shadow
Falls over you: above the surface,
The figure of Sleep
Has leaned over its boat.
Hear Sleep's feet plop in the shallows——
It pulls the boat to shore.

On a Cold Day in Late March, Near Easter

I took the car through turns, down long roads,
along wood fences, and saw horses, just two,
far off, in a field. One turned its head toward me——
the other stood motionless so long
I began to wonder whether it was real or a fake
put there to keep the other company,
until finally it bowed its head
earthward. Farther on, I saw a flock of small birds
pulsing together as points over the brown grass,
like tiny buoys responding to air currents,
rising and dipping, the air moving
the smallest feathers on their bellies.

Empty Coats

An empty coat
moves down a street of pot-holes, the sleeves
wrapped around a sack of groceries.
At the edge of the block, the empty coat
shrinks to a pin-prick,
then vanishes
around the corner——to meet
another empty coat. They open their sleeves
for a good-bye hug,
and everything falls to the ground.

After My Parents Divorced

I drove past the old house. At dusk,
it was blue, all the green things
in the yard unearthed, and dirt
with huge boulders. It appeared to me
like a photographic print——thin
paper washed in the blue-colored, watery
tray, held up, dim, dripping,
by tongs. I thought of the words: *gene pool.*
My white hands, curled around
the black steering wheel, were almost blue.
The bones looked thin, watery,
about to evaporate.

In Late Spring

We drove north, past the point
where leafed-trees turn to pine, back to where
we learned to swim together in the lake.
We'd just learned Mom and Dad were separating.
From shore, between trees, I watched you
breast-stroke across——the bobbing
of your copper head in a sheet of blue
made concentric rings that grew smaller,
to a pin-point, then vanished.
I waited——on the horizon,
the lake was the same as before,
Sister: the clear water, noiseless
sheet of glass bordered by pines.
It seemed to me a continent, its own
tectonic plate shifting on the globe.
At last your head appeared to me, across
the water, growing larger, out of the lake
like a rising sun, and out
of the icy water you climbed, radiant,
and strong body showered with drops.

Walking with My Sister

It's on a walk in Stony Creek
My sister's steps print next to me,

And she is watching blades of grass
Bend in the wind and part at last——

But I watch our foot prints roll down
That shaded path, a crunching sound:

How singular and gray they are,
Each grain pressed still under our marks.

III

The Oldest, Wordless Story

Feeling wordless, yet urgent, I write to you
to try to tell you something——
this wordlessness
is part of the illness, the real nausea,
the deep, palpable sickness I feel
in my body. It has something to do
with the body, in fact. It has
to do with women and men
and the individual bodies
and the relations between them.
The separateness, the limitations;
the inescapable, rooted urges——
the impossible, sabotaging urges
developed and deepened horribly
from the beginning of time.
Feeling this way, one day, having just
had sex with a man, having just
felt once again, again and again,
the palpitations hidden in my own dark core,
I was hungry, and so I went
inside a Chinese restaurant.
Waiting for my food, I watched
a tank full of enormous carp,
circling in the water, opening and closing
the O's of their mouths.
I wished to God they would stop
making those silent O's at me.
Shut up, I thought. One fish
held my long stare: a huge carp, entirely white,
every scale white, with one eye missing

and just a white hole instead. I asked
about the fish, and the workers told me
it was sick, and had poked its eye out
on an object in the tank——they'd heard
a POP! and went to look, and there
was blood streaming from the socket.
Sick, I waited for my food
and watched the carp, that horrible
huge sick fish with a no-eye, an empty
white socket, slowly circling the tank,
opening and closing the O of its mouth——

In the Darkness, Pigeon-Sex

It is late. I am a woman
lying alone on my bed,
impossibly awake, sickened
to my core about sex. My limbs
are piled at various angles
on these silver sheets, and the fucking
pigeons are thick in my eaves,
on my roof, everywhere around me
outside my room, insisting
on their awful sex-noises.

I want for this single moment
to feel asexual, to pretend
there is no sex, to sleep.
I smother the flame of the candle
on my bedside table:
the wax on my finger burns.

Still, they layer their pulsed throat-throbs,
insist, increase, start low
and climb, in convulsive
throat-lunges, calling me
to the alarmed state of remaining
conscious and sexed and sick.

Quill Tip, Ink Well

A peacock
rounded the bed: plucked
long entrails   from my belly—

A child
in a yellow coat
stood in the doorway to see.

The light patter:
    its little feet
continued inside sleep   and out
of this, out of this
came words   from me:
I never loved you   I said.

The stars went on
dripping their milk:

Johannes, You Seem Confused

after Johannes Bobrowski's poem,
"The Bird, White"

about your Bird, White. I too
have a dead white bird
in my life, and I too
have mixed feelings. You'd think
I'd be wholly and purely
filled with joy at the loss
of that albatross——then
why do I still mourn?
It was a thing that was supposed to be
ideal. And built to last,
supernally.
It's over.
Totaled.
Dead. But it was never hung,
it never had a funeral.
Unsung,
above the milk suns.
And a wheel
turns, terrible,
to crush it in the stars.

I Gave Him Back His Roses

I gave myself some good advice: I exited
the infrastructure. I fled, saying,
Detach, Detach——the Safety Latch
and flipped the lid of my little box,
and once inside, I got the clamp snapped shut. It is
a little room cramped with mirrors.
I don't know where they came from,
the cuts and all
the bruises——were they from before?
Or are they from the mirrors' exposed
edges? All day, the bruises congeal
like darkening clouds around their blood clots.
My fingers point into the mirrors——I accuse myself.
Above the black hood, the camera's flashbulb pops:
an eclipse of light——
I am the No One's Rose.

Sophie at the Ashcan

Sophie at the ashcan
       where bats dove down
Standing in her smudged apron
       between wires in the air,
Wringing her hands in cloth
       snatching things in their mouths
And saying—*No there is nothing there*
       inside that box that is cold
No there is nothing at all
       where ice-plums drop from the ceiling
Eyeing the melons on the counter
       where air shunts in from one corner
Feeling—I am a prisoner
       the wires swinging from pulleys
Saying—*I hope to be a Dangerous Beastie*
       swooping down into the box,
And sharpen my knives in Calcutta
       catching Sophie

Danger: Some Questions

Everyone is dangerous. Sex?
Dangerous. Dark and scary.
Is it always? Is it the pit
of life itself? Can it ever be light?
Can a core, a deep groove,
ever be light? Where's the fissure——
a crack in the tooth, a crease
in the brain, a sex-fold——that's light?

In the bookstore restroom, Danger:
there's a woman in a wheelchair
unable to maneuver into the dark stall.
She needs the help of the upright stranger. She
is red-faced, rapidly thanking. Oh, unzip
the pants, oh-sorry elbows hitting
metal stall walls. Cramped. Slid,
somehow, onto the toilet. Oh. Thank you.

The Anatomy of Hiding

She walks around outside in the world, hiding
the teeth she'd gnash at any threat——
say, that tart at the party last weekend——with a smile, or with
the lips closed over them. She hides
the perceptions, taken in through the holes——
the sex-hole, eye-holes, ear and nose-holes, mouth and even pore
holes——then the brain-signals: feelings, thoughts,
then words, down in the abdomen, almost touching
the uterus, lodging
over the stomach near the heart,
not even so far as the trachea, the larynx
or the back of the throat, where would tremble
the vocal chords, where notes, meaning things, would fill
the space of the mouth, before entering
the air out there beyond the edge
of the teeth, and float towards his ears——

Death by Tricycle

The way she died, one day,
was that she was hit
by a tricycle. They say
she was delirious, smitten

by the light of the sun
banking off the ice-cream truck,
or by an idea to run
after the vision of Love. Struck!

Silent Comments at the Funeral of a Secret Crush

Erotic love depends on distance——so,
this is perfect! Your bones are laid out
in such white finery, and I
am a stranger to everyone here.
Earlier, I overheard
your mother giving out
her secret recipe for lemon-
rind cake, the sugar tang that made
your red lips pucker. I stole it.

IV

Trip to the World

Let's all go to the hospital,
Let's all hold hands,
Let's all go to the hospital, holding hands,

It's a trip to the world,
It's a trip with your friends,
And it may hurt, dears, but it ends,

So take your little hankies,
And take your little bones,
And link them each to each, the hospital is home,

They'll tag us and they'll feed us
Like the little birds we are,
We'll have bright colored bands on our cold little feet,

They'll teach us to walk,
To sleep and to talk,
They'll teach us to scrawl with our scrawny hands,

So let's go, let's go to the hospital,
Let's all hold hands,
Let's go to the hospital, holding hands——

Rondel of the Woman in a Hospital Bed

The surgeon's eye looks into mine,
the fluorescent light halos his head.
I fall asleep, and still I see my bed,
my body there, the gray-clothed forms like mimes

around me, watching the surgeon slice
inside my mouth. His hands are red.
The surgeon's eye looks into mine;
the fluorescent light halos his head

as he stitches the cuts with fishing line.
I am hungry. I want to be fed
plums. I am hooked up with tubes, instead.
My bruises throb: I wake to find
the surgeon's eye looks into mine.

Picture of a Falling Head with Open Mouth

Mouth-hole, key-hole:
the silent scream, slipping
down——
like a parade of long, red
fire engines, lights flashing,
no sound.

To Will:

Well! Here we are together, all alone.
You look a little white, but not angry.
With that loop of rope around your neck, the hole
of your mouth, stunned, you look struck by fear.
You're pinned neatly in this tree——Whoosh! Wings
flush out in the distant woods, a blue

sound. You know, in the pre-dawn light, everything is blue.
It reminds me of a time I woke up alone,
barefoot, in the woods. I'd been sleepwalking. The sound of wings
woke me up. First I was startled, then angry
at myself for panicking: I was lost with no light. Fear
choked me. How would I find my way home? Holes

in the black sky made chinks of light between pines. Holes
in the ground were visible now: my footprints, blue
in the damp earth. I followed them home without fear.
Will, are you afraid of being alone?
I must admit I feel a little angry
seeing you hanging here. Are you listening? Wings

are pulsing everywhere. Inside us, beyond us, wings
are thundering. I imagine you now in a kind of hole,
a vacuum, no light, no sound, but full of anger.
Do you remember the time I turned blue?
When I woke up, my chest felt bruised. I was alone;
I couldn't breathe. The world of my mind turned white with fear.

I went to the emergency room where doctors thrushed with fear
like birds in their white coats, fluttering their wings
around the x-rays. They left me on the steel table alone
while they chittered among themselves. I felt myself sink in a hole
of white light, until I was aware of nothing. Blue,
when I woke up. Blue veins, blue gown, blue tube. Angry

wings above my head. White light, pixels of angry
light thrashing madly. The tube was a plastic hole, like fear
running air into my lung, tissue paper, blue,
saying yes pink, saying no blue, my lungs, like wings
catching new wind, my delicate, flimsy hole,
and low and behold I was still alive and alone.

When they beat their angry wings,
do you feel fear inside your hole?
You bastard, I'm blue, and alone.

Panic

Night rain falls on grass
in the still cemetery
where moths still flicker.

By Little

When you lose so much, it is like this:
You search, the way you search the mirror
for home but do not find it——
the way you search the insides
of the building where you can be alone
but do not find it, home. And so,
you avoid them, the things
that should be home, but aren't——
apart, separate even from your body,
you search outwards, far, at night,
in your car, where you are found
by little white wings startled in your headlights
and stunned on your windshield.

Driving North for Consolation

Through the ice-crystalled windshield, the sun
just up and white, small trees
are covered with ice—
their tiny branches are weighted with it;
they move in the wind but do not break.

Inside the car, the hands are blue-white
and numb, wrapped around the steering wheel,
while the smell of exhaust mingles with the taste
of a cold tongue and toothpaste—
the engine drones; the wind screams.

Celan's Deathfugue

Drown the mouth-hole
Drown and Drown it
In the River there in the River
Where earless, eyeless, perfectly
Voiceless the Pulley
Cranks over the Water
The Pulley-Wheel, the sleepless
Unblinking eye, over which
The Wire runs, the Wire to
No One,
The Faceless Hand
Over the Black Water,
Pulling and Pulling to Drown
The eye-hole, mouth-hole,
The No-One's key-hole——

The Possum

You're rolling the wheels
of the grocery cart
fast over the asphalt
to put food in the car.

You're driving the car
with the food in the back
over the black hills
turned white in the headlights.

You pass the house
and keep on driving
with the music on
because you're lonely.

A possum waddles
into the road, huge
and white, frozen
on its pink feet,

Eyes fixed in the light.
You stop, the possum
nearly under the tire,
the oranges flying forward.

The possum heads back
for the cattails. It glances
at you over its shoulder,
and looks disappointed.

In the Kitchen at the Restaurant

for Tim McCoy

The head chef
kept a glass-doored fridge
just for dessert ingredients.
Once, I saw
a clear bucket—huge!—
full of eggs,
just the insides, without
their shells: yellow yolk-sacs
floating in their whites. The big bang
went off inside my skull
and it was a million suns
suspended in a bucket,
the primordial ooze
of first life in dark water,
the eggs waiting in a womb,
and a memory came to me
of a phone call with a friend
who was in the middle
of relating his suicide attempt
when my cell's battery died
and cut the connection
leaving the sound of static
and my imagination of frayed wires——

Moussaoui's Mother

after the trial of Zacarias Moussaoui, attended by his mother

Moussaoui, Moussaoui—saying the name this way, becomes
Beautiful—
Like paper mâché, a wet cloth, molding a face—
Or a moth, hovering over, or smothering, the lips—
Moussaoui—another created creature—
All those choices, a lattice of water—
Moussaoui—think of a brain, its slippery folds—
Moussaoui, a new person-form, a human-form
Of Origami.

Menopausal Pantoum

Nearing Easter, purple begins to appear
everywhere. And eggs: anything remotely
round—a clay pot, a mouth-hole, a tear—
reminds her of an egg. The warm, earthy,

everywhere eggs—but she remains remote.
In the grocery store, her steel-toed boots
remind her of eggs; but instead of warm earth,
they hit hard linoleum, and she hears ghosts

in the grocery store, between steel-toed boot-
strikes, of all her unborn children. The children
hit hard linoleum, and she hears their ghosts
like menstrual flow slipping past her. She listens

to the strikes of all her unborn children:
round, like clay pots, like mouth-holes, tears,
like menstrual flow slipping past her. She listens
to nearing Easter, as purple begins to appear.

Boys Leave the Farm at Dawn to Fight in the Civil War

The blue animals
move calmly over the soil,
hair combed, parted straight——

wade silently——long
arms of wheat, unharvested,
part down the earth's scalp.

Dead Too Soon

The dead are up; they're down
there again, making a fuss:
the old man's stomping around,
shouting about all the dust.

Tonight it's the same old tune——
the clarinets are in the corner;
the kid wails on the bassoon.
This gig's getting older and older.

V

The Pigeons

In the pale blue half-light
between bad dreams and waking,
a slight music enters, lighter,
some peace drifting softly down
in throat-fluttered notes. The quiet whir
of wings, this chorus of muses,
urging me to wake, take heart, to
breathe——to fill my lungs with air——

View from a Sleep-Deprived Early-Morning Dog-Walker

Everything's okay
with you and the world
when your eyes stay open
in the dark all night——
two little planets
orbiting with the other constellations
tracing various shapes
in your convoluted network
of dendrites and axons, and when
at five a.m., your room is lit
with the moon of your sister's face,
saying, get up, it's time
to walk the dogs——
so you go, shuffling in slippers
with fleece and scarf and hat
down the street, with the well-
rested dog at the end
of your leash, burrowing
and exploding from heaps of leaves,
like sunbursts of joy, over
and over, bounding
and boundless, lighting
the pre-sunrise morning——

Salon

sitting in the hair salon, waiting
for my turn to get a hair cut,
looking around me: women
tugging their hair, making a fuss

(it's their turn to get hair cuts):
they complain about their faces,
tugging their hair, making a fuss,
trying to make it work, making

complaints about their faces,
all talk, lights, movement, all swiftness,
trying to make it work, making
so much effort, and color, worry, less

talk, lights, movement, and swiftness:
magazines, piles, beauty and fashion
with so much effort, color, worry, less—
but one National Geographic: inside

the magazine, piles of beauty and fashion:
the big face of a water buffalo—
in one National Geographic, inside,
her eyelashes lit up in sun,

the big face of the water buffalo,
flecked with wet mud, her liquid eyes,
her eyelashes lit up in sun,
looking into my soft face:

flecked with wet mud, her liquid eyes
intense as these women in the salon
looking into me, our soft faces,
as we are alone, as we are one:

intense as these women in the salon
looking around me: women
alone, as we are one
sitting in the hair salon, waiting.

It Was a Day in Florence Near One Replica of David

I saw a fair-skinned human
cross the street.

There was so much
exhaust,
and the neck
was exposed:
flesh, tender
and throbbing.

Baptism

When I stand at the kitchen sink
and let the warm water
run in a stream
into my cupped hands
I hear wings, sifting,
flutter of the tongue on its palate.
The bird curves its belly into my palm,
flickers its wings in the bath,
dipping its head under sometimes,
then preens its specter feathers of light
in quick bows and turns.

The Animal that Lives in Fire

The Animal that Lives in Fire
is a shape I make out in the tile
on the bathroom floor.
Inside the strawberry,
at the center of the Earth,
inside the First Cherokee
is the Animal that Lives in Fire.
Embedded in the pages of the book
my lover reads
is the Animal that Lives in Fire.
It looks out from the windows
of our nonexistence;
it wipes the salt from its lips.
Before us, and after us:
the Animal that Lives in Fire.

Zoo Animals in the Rain

We dressed our bodies in clothes we bought at a store.
We put makeup on each others' faces and we went to the zoo.

The zoo animals like church lights in the rain:
The zoo animals in their furred feet, wet heads
Licking their faces into shapes:

Blurred, rain on glass:

The zoo animals' eyes in the rain, their eyes
Look out of cages, into ours, out of cages, looking back:
We shuffle in our furs. We shuffle
and look out of cages—

The zoo animals' voices in the rain:
We murmur and rub against ourselves.

There is a bevel, there is a pedestal.
There is a fountain, there is a font.

We come to this point. We all
Come to this point, where we call
And shuffle, and murmur, among, against,
Ourselves.

The zoo animals like church lights in the rain
Of red candles, eyes of red lights in windows,
Furred feet, wet heads—

Acknowledgments

Grateful acknowledgment is made to the editors of the following chapbook and journals, in which many of these poems originally appeared:

Zoo Animals in the Rain – a chapbook of poems. Philadelphia, Pennsylvania: Turtle Ink Press, 2009.

The Alembic: "Making My World of Cut-Paper Dolls," "The Monarch"

The Barefoot Muse: "Menopausal Pantoum"

Barrow Street: "Johannes, You Seem Confused"

Coevolution 2, an Anthology: "Moussaoui's Mother"

Comstock Review: "Blood, Glass, Pigeons in the Bathtub," "the Relativity of Nothing," "The Sparrow," "What is a Woman"

H_NGM_N: "View from an Early-Morning Sleep-Deprived Dog-Walker"

Partners for Arts Education: "Red Balloon"

The Pedestal Magazine: "The Oldest, Wordless Story"

Poets for Living Waters: "The Animal that Lives in Fire," "By Little," "Celan's Deathfugue"

POOL: "Silent Comments at the Funeral of a Secret Crush"

Redactions: Poetry & Poetics: "To Will"

Skive: "Baptism"

Slush Pile: "Sophie at the Ashcan"

Stone Canoe: "April Heat," "Boys Leave the Farm at Dawn to Fight in the Civil War," "There," "Zoo Animals in the Rain"

Two Rivers Review: "The Possum"

Vitruvius: "Anorexia," "Empty Coats," "The End of Sleep,"
    "Reflective," "Rondel of the Woman in a Hospital Bed"

"Boys Leave the Farm at Dawn to Fight in the Civil War" was set to
    music for choir by Edward Ruchalski.

"The Monarch" was set to music for piano by Edward Ruchalski.

"There" was included as a recording of Elizabeth Twiddy's voice
    in the film *A Resonant Chord: Rodger Mack and the Creative Process*,
    directed by Linda M. Herbert, Syracuse Alternative Media
    Network, 2009.

Thanks to the spirits who've guided me in writing these poems.

Thanks to all my teachers: Jim Brasfield, Bruce Weigl, Brooks
Haxton, Bruce Smith, Chris Kennedy, Michael Burkard, and
Mary Karr, along with Alice Fulton and Rhina Espaillat, for
giving so generously of their time and care.

Thanks to Bob Colley, Philippe Pascal, and Adam Rozum for
publishing and designing this book——and for being people
outside of myself who became invested in this work.

Thanks to my family and to my husband, Edward Ruchalski,
whose love and dedication saw me through the dark into the light,
making this book possible.

About the Author

Elizabeth Twiddy won The Joyce Carol Oates Award for Poetry from Syracuse University, and her chapbook, *Zoo Animals in the Rain* (Turtle Ink Press, 2009), includes several poems that have been nominated for Pushcart Prizes. Most recently, her poems have appeared in *Barrow Street, POOL, The Alembic, H_NGM_N,* the Australian journal *Skive,* and elsewhere. She is on faculty, teaching poetry workshops and literature courses at the Syracuse YMCA's Downtown Writer's Center and serves as an editor for the poetry journal *Comstock Review.*

Twiddy holds degrees in Biochemistry and Chemistry from The Pennsylvania State University at University Park, where she designed and synthesized a molecule that aids in cancer detection. She began a Ph.D. in Pharmacology at Yale, then worked in research laboratories at the Dartmouth College Medical School before earning her MFA in Poetry at Syracuse University. She has taught writing and literature at SUNY College of Environmental Science and Forestry, and at Le Moyne College, and has worked with students in the Syracuse City Schools on numerous projects, including the U.S. Poet Laureate Project, Literacy through Creative Expression. She lives in Syracuse, New York with her husband, the composer Edward Ruchalski, who has set a number of her poems to music for choir and for piano. For more, visit elizabethtwiddy.com.

Praise for *Love-Noise*

The electricity here has such an incandescence, it could be resurgent voltage from Emily Dickinson in distress. Even where the simplest language comes straight on, the cadence is the core of the effect. Twiddy's handling of inflection, in image and in sound, makes poems come alive. A wasp, a pigeon, an opossum, any animal in these poems is the anima revealed, the soul, an apparition—maybe winged, but not because it is transcendent: it is always the genuine psyche, fraught with all the freight of flesh and mind. What haunts the whole book, in the surge and aftermath of eros, in the empathy for family and for strangers, and in jolts of recognition, and of being recognized, is an imagination deeply and disturbingly alive, and tender to the touch.

— Brooks Haxton

In these severely attenuated poems come urgent transmissions. The poems derive from the hidden and secret, take place on the verge of silence and make us lean in closer to listen. Elizabeth Twiddy prefers the small spaces: boxes, bedrooms, hospitals, brain and sex folds, eye and mouth holes. In the small spaces seismic movements happen that have the power to unsettle us as good poems do. And we are constantly rubbed against by the animal: the sparrow, pigeon, wasp, horse, peacock, moth, dog and those that are not quite human and not quite other. What we hear in these poems is a noise both strange and subtle—fascinating, inexplicable, beautiful.

— Bruce Smith

One of the many strengths of this remarkable collection of poems is its capacity to engage, move, amuse, delight and frighten all at the same time, often within the same poem. More than once I found myself laughing over some situation that also broke my heart—reading "Danger: Some Questions," for instance, in which the vulnerability of the body is treated with loving, unsentimental intelligence—or shocked by a poem that also aroused unexpected sorrow, such as "Moussaoui's Mother." If intelligence is, in part, the ability to deal with ambiguity without losing any of the conflicting flavors of reality, these poems have it in spades.

They also have a playful dark humor that pretends to make light of very serious themes by means of sometimes outrageous metaphors, extreme situations used to frame what is not being said directly, and an aggressive, almost visionary surrealism that captures the reader's attention at once, and focuses it firmly. I've been returning, with pleasure and a frisson of anxiety, to such poems as "Empty Coats," "Picture of a Falling Head with Open Mouth," and the stunning "The Animal that Lives in Fire."

And finally, for a formal poet like me, there is a special joy in finding, among these excellent free verse poems, several others that surprise by using such forms as the haiku, pantoum, triolet, sestina and rondel, not always with the decorous respect usually accorded them, but irreverently—and with a brazen kind of success.

— Rhina P. Espaillat